BACKSTAGE

BACK

TEXT AND PHOTOGRAPHS BY PIERRE PETITJEAN

TEXT TRANSLATED BY
Jeannette and Richard Seaver

PENGUIN BOOKS

PENGUIN BOOKS

BACKSTAGE

Before discovering photography, which changed his life "like a thunderbolt," Pierre Petitjean wanted to be an airline pilot. Shortly thereafter, he fell in love with dance, and since that time he has photographed many of the leading ballet companies in the world, including the Ballet Théâtre Contemporain, the Ballet du Grand Théâtre de Genève, the Ballet Théâtre Polonais, the American Ballet Theatre, and the New York City Ballet. A professional photographer for a dozen years, he has published photographs in *L'Express, Le Point, Elle, Le Figaro, Le Nouvel Observateur, Dance, Vogue Italie,* and many other magazines and newspapers. His travels have taken him to Lebanon, Syria, Jordan, the United States, Poland, and most of Europe. He makes his home in Angers, France, where he lives with his wife, Colette, and three children, Stéphane, Julien, and Anne-Sophie.

STAGE
With the Ballet

Penguin Books Ltd, Harmondsworth,
Middlesex, England
Penguin Books, 625 Madison Avenue,
New York, New York 10022, U.S.A.
Penguin Books Australia Ltd, Ringwood,
Victoria, Australia
Penguin Books Canada Limited, 2801 John Street,
Markham, Ontario, Canada L3R 1B4
Penguin Books (N.Z.) Ltd, 182–190 Wairau Road,
Auckland 10, New Zealand

First published in the United States of America by
The Viking Press (A Seaver Book) 1978
Published in Penguin Books 1979

LIBRARY OF CONGRESS CATALOGING IN PUBLICATION DATA
Petitjean, Pierre, 1947–
  Backstage.
  1. Ballet. I. Title.
[GV1787.P4813 1979]   792.8   79-11514
ISBN 0 14 00.5185 6

Printed in the United States of America by
The Murray Printing Company, Westford, Massachusetts
Set in Linotype Fairfield

I dedicate this book especially to her who shares my strange and peripatetic life, to my children, and also to Paul Lepercq.

I sincerely thank all the dancers who have kindly allowed me to photograph them through the years, and especially those whose photographs appear in this volume, all members of the following companies: the New York City Ballet, the American Ballet Theatre, the Ballet du Grand Théâtre de Genève, and the Ballet Théâtre Contemporain. Thanks also to the directors and administrators of these companies who allowed me to work in the intimacy of their respective backstages. I am, finally, especially grateful to Patricia Neary and François Letaconnoux, whose precious help and collaboration made this book possible.

The true origins of this book go back several years, to my hometown of Angers, France. Whether or not photography would become a way of life for me I did not know, but by the time I was eighteen I had already begun free-lancing for local theater and opera groups, essentially promotion and publicity work. Then one day in 1970 a nationally subsidized touring dance company—the Ballet Théâtre Contemporain—stopped in Angers. One of my friends who had seen the company rehearse was enthusiastic and urged me to take a look for myself. With camera in hand, I went to the theater, to the wings and backstage area with which I was already familiar, and there, in the short span of a few hours, I had what I can only call an "illumination": I fell in love with the dance.

One of my three sisters had studied ballet, and I had always regarded dancing as something rather silly, and especially "unmasculine." No longer. I watched with growing awe the grace and beauty of the different dancers, the magical coordination with which they moved and intertwined, formed and re-formed patterns that even to my untutored eye were intricate yet sublimely simple.

The company stayed three days in Angers, and for three days I photographed. After each day's rehearsal I hurried home, worked late into the night developing and printing what I had shot. The next morning I took what I thought were my best prints and showed them to the dancers. They liked what they saw and urged me to take more. By the time the company moved on, I had already accumulated a variety of photographs of the ballet. As I look back on them, they display a naïveté and amateurism in the light of what I now know about the dance, but they remain my children, and I do not disown them. All those pictures, I might add, were taken not backstage but from the more conventional angles: photos of dancers onstage, taken from the auditorium.

In France there is an annual prize—or fellowship—for black-and-white photography, and one day I decided to assemble my best ballet pictures and submit them. I knew there were three thousand contestants. No matter. What did I have to lose? As it turned out, my positive attitude paid off: I won the prize, and with the money in hand set off almost immediately for Iran. I spent several weeks there taking photographs, and when I returned to France I sold the photo-documentary to a magazine. With these two "commercial

successes" behind me, any vacillation about my future as a professional photographer vanished, and I set up shop in Angers.

Not long afterward, the Ballet Théâtre Contemporain was given a home base—Angers. The director, remembering my earlier work, called and asked if I would become the company's official photographer. After two or three seconds' hesitation, I accepted. From that day on, my love affair with ballet really bloomed.

My main job was to photograph the principal dancers, in classic poses and movements, for use on programs, posters, and advertisements. But between official takes I often wandered backstage, and soon I found myself taking more pictures there than of performances. I never stopped to analyze why; but I now realize that this "other life" of the dance, this world of grueling work and endless rehearsal, of informality and relaxation and, yes, even of boredom, seduced my photographer's eye.

The director of the Ballet Théâtre Contemporain invited other dance companies to Angers, not only French but also foreign groups; before long I was photographing them as well—most often from the classical onstage angles, for that is what the companies wanted, and that was what they paid for: a marvelous leap, a graceful arabesque, all lighted in some subtle way to bring out the most dramatic effect. By now I knew ballet well enough so that I could foresee movements, anticipate climaxes, and react quickly, often under trying circumstances. But I could not help feeling that in all these pictures I was just an "intellectual click," an earnest technician, whereas by definition the dance is a world of sensibility and sensitivity, where the soul is touched, and where one has the feeling, however fleeting, that one can create. And the more I saw and studied dance, the more I became convinced that it was in the other world, the one hidden behind the sophisticated smiles of the stage, that I might uncover the true soul of ballet: the world I call "backstage."

For me the term encompasses more than the wings and corridors behind the stage: I see backstage also as the stage itself during rehearsal, and all the classes and studio rehearsals that are the dancer's lot throughout his life. I love the ballet seen from the auditorium—the spectacle, the glamour, and beauty of performance—for that, really, is what dance is all about. But I love even more the hidden face of the planet "dance," the side the public rarely sees.

In this universe, where all the joys and miseries alike are visible, though not so openly as in life, a climate of beauty envelops the feelings, which are always—or so it seems to me—acute. Sensibilities are bared, but the spirit is such that they blossom, not wither, in this rarefied world, where spontaneity and musicality reign.

The conjunction of the very special, almost unreal light of the rehearsal halls and the fabulous plasticity of the dancers themselves is what I have tried to convey in my photographs. Here there are no restrictions; here, at last, I have the freedom to express myself, to look and choose at will, never to submit.

The camera is nothing more than a cumbersome appendage. . . .

The performance lasts three hours. Backstage lasts months, years, a lifetime, and that life is a succession of efforts—courage, will, pain, solitude, anguish, frustration, joy—all bathed in an atmosphere that exists nowhere else.

It is this universe "backstage"—which despite differences of geography remains somehow the same, whether in Paris or New York, London or Moscow—that I have seen and loved, and have done my best to transpose onto the pages that follow.

Angers, 1978

P. P.

BACKSTAGE

Shoes. I have always been surprised by the number of pairs of shoes that ballet dancers use. The brand-new ones shown top left are Patricia McBride's, stored in her dressing room. She, like most principal ballerinas, uses a new pair for each performance. Why? Because the rigors of the dance "break" the shoes. But that does not mean they are then discarded; on the contrary, they are kept as practice slippers. Top right are several pairs of Gelsey Kirkland's practice slippers, lined up backstage while Miss Kirkland rehearses. Lower left, Cynthia Harvey laces up her shoes. Lower right, Elizabeth Ashton in the fourth position.

Jolinda Menendez, a soloist with the American Ballet Theatre. I have photographed her dozens of times, and always, in every shot, there appears a feeling of sadness and melancholy. Her fellow dancers assured me that Jolinda, far from being sad, is full of gaiety and life.

This picture was taken in the cupola of the Paris Opéra, which was put at the disposal of the American Ballet Theatre for rehearsal purposes when it came to Paris in 1977.

In the morning, before rehearsals, there are classes to limber up and loosen the muscles. Tradition has it that the dancers all start at the *barre*, and follow prescribed movements and exercises under the tutelage of a coach. Gelsey Kirkland, a principal ballerina of the American Ballet Theatre, has her own personal method. But once she is warmed up, she rejoins the class.

Gelsey Kirkland. Arabesque. Here again, while her colleagues follow traditional and time-honored methods, Gelsey is guided by her own muse. Paris, 1976.

Cynthia Harvey, of the American Ballet Theatre. This shot was taken when the company performed in Paris in 1976. Performances took place in the gardens of the Louvre, but classes and rehearsals were held in the Paris Opéra—more precisely in the beautiful studio in the cupola of the opera.

Janet Shibata, of the American Ballet Theatre, during a class. Classes generally consist of two parts: warm-up exercises at the *barre* to loosen the muscles; dance exercises without support of the *barre*. Here, Janet is in phase two, exercising with Eric Nesbitt, of the same company. Note that Janet is wearing a rubber suit, the purpose of which is to keep the dancer's muscles from tightening up. Paris Opéra, 1976.

A practice session at the Paris Opéra. I have rarely seen mattresses backstage, but one day at the cupola rehearsal area one appeared, and here three dancers of the American Ballet Theatre wasted no time taking advantage of its comforts.

Janet Shibata, during a break. I was taken by the beauty of Janet's contemplative pose, the extraordinary light filtering in from the streets, and the dilapidated state of the old walls of the Paris Opéra. I had a feeling I had transcended both geography and time, and that this was a nineteenth-century Japanese woodblock print I was looking at. Paris, 1976.

Jolinda Menendez, still in a pensive mood, resting between classes. Her resting place here is under the rehearsal piano in the practice studio of the Paris Opéra. 1976.

There is something gracefully feline about the dance; and dancers, I have found, often naturally assume poses and seek places of repose where one might expect to find a cat.

Close-up of hands during *barre* exercises. . . .

A fuller view of dancers of the American Ballet Theatre exercising at the *barre*. In the foreground, Yoko Morishita, one of the company's principal dancers.

Feet and legs, exercising at the *barre*.

Reflected view of members of the Ballet
Théâtre Contemporain warming up in Angers,
France, home base of the company. I liked the
sparseness, even the coldness, of this modern
architecture, which was symbolized for me by
the image of the five dancers in the mirror.

Dancers of the American Ballet Theatre during a class. Three distinctly different yet typical movements. Here again the diffused light of the rehearsal studio bathed the dancers and lent them an ethereal grace.

A class of the American Ballet Theatre. At first glance regimentation seems to prevail, but a closer look reveals that each dancer's sensibility is at work.

Close-up of feet, wrapped in woolen leg-warmers. In the years I have watched dancers' feet, I have often thought that if those feet could talk . . .

Members of the American Ballet Theatre relaxing during a class in their studio. After the arduous exercises, the dancers have to unwind, but they also must make sure their muscles don't tighten up, so they proceed to a series of stretching exercises tailored to their own needs. Like all athletes, dancers are acutely conscious of their bodies, and I am convinced that dancers are more self-conscious than anyone. To be able to use their bodies at full capacity, day after day, with the least effort to produce the maximum expression, dancers have an intimate awareness of their every muscle and bone and nerve, from the tips of their fingers to their toes.

Marianna Tcherkassky, a principal dancer of
the American Ballet Theatre, relaxing during
a class.

It was a freezing day, and the only place one could keep one's muscles warm, during a break in class, was where I found this dancer of the American Ballet Theatre. Here is another example of the feline pose. New York, winter 1977.

Two dancers of the American Ballet Theatre during a break in class. Dance is all-consuming, and I have never seen any artist work harder than a dancer to maintain or improve his or her level of performance. But even dancers need time for romance.

Alina Hernandez, of the American Ballet
Theatre. New York, 1977.

Marianna Tcherkassky. During a break in her own class, Marianna stepped over to watch her colleagues rehearsing in another studio, and I caught this double image of her, since she is actually watching the other class in the mirror. Though she looks asleep, she is not; she is simply captivated by the group's feet.

Gelsey Kirkland and Ivan Nagy, two principal dancers of the American Ballet Theatre, rehearsing *Giselle*. New York, 1977.

Gelsey Kirkland after a rehearsal. Even for
the greatest stars, all is not smiles, bows, and
standing ovations. Here I was struck not only
by the bleakness of the setting but by the
feeling of fatigue and loneliness that Gelsey
seemed to reflect in this pose. And I was re-
minded once again of the endless, back-
breaking work, the total commitment that is
part and parcel of the dancer's life.

Stephanie Saland, of the New York City
Ballet, before a class. Paris, November 1976.

Stephanie Saland, rummaging in her bag during a class break. When I saw this pose, I realized that we common mortals, in a like situation, would have bent down to rummage. Not so with ballet dancers. . . .

Stephanie Saland just before a daily class.
Paris, 1977.

The intense activity typifies a backstage just before daily classes. The dancers are into their individual routines, some already warming up, others checking to make sure their shoes have enough rosin to prevent slipping, others merely chatting prior to warming up. For me, this picture sums up the whole world of backstage that for years I have been pursuing and recording. The New York City Ballet, Paris, 1976.

Mikhail Barishnikov rehearsing Balanchine's ballet *Prodigal Son*.

Mobility and immobility. Two members of
the New York City Ballet, during a rehearsal.
Paris, 1976.

Jerome Robbins, one of the two emperors of
the dance, watching a rehearsal of the New
York City Ballet. Paris, 1976.

Members of the New York City Ballet. Three favorite backstage pastimes of dancers when they are not rehearsing or exercising: sewing, chatting, and reading. And sometimes a fourth: knitting.

Susan Freedman, of the New York City Ballet. Dancers have a natural beauty of movement and pose, but here I was especially struck not only by the grace of line but also by the extreme beauty of the subject.

Linda Homek, of the New York City Ballet. Another example of the striking beauty of a dancer's pose, caught in a very special light. Paris, 1976.

Members of the American Ballet Theatre relaxing after a rehearsal in the beautiful setting
of the Louvre's outdoor theater.

Members of the New York City Ballet watching a rehearsal of a ballet with music by Brahms, at the Théâtre des Champs-Élysées. The simple beauty of the several dancers at rest caught my eye. They are not actually all at rest, however, as again the three favorite backstage pastimes—reading, sewing, and small talk—occupy some. Paris, November 1976.

Eleanor D'Antuono, a principal dancer of the American Ballet Theatre, here looking like a marionette offstage. Taken at the New York City Center Theater, during a rehearsal of *Giselle*. There are in the American Ballet Theatre several couples of principal dancers who alternately dance the same role. They all rehearse together, and here Eleanor watches while another dancer takes her turn.

Marie Johansson, of the American Ballet Theatre, during an afternoon rehearsal in the open-air theater constructed in the spring of 1977 in the courtyard of the Louvre. I was struck here by the contrast between the seventeenth-century architecture and the twentieth-century pose.

Mikhail Baryshnikov during a rehearsal of the American Ballet Theatre's *Don Quixote*, with Natalia Makarova, on the immense outdoor stage of the Louvre. However much he may look like a latter-day Sampson, here Mikhail is not bringing down the columns of the museum, for what his outstretched arms are touching is actually a stage set, a replica of the stones of the Louvre, and the door on the left is really a sliding door. Inside the Louvre, in the spring of 1977, a huge amphitheater was built at one end of the courtyard, with a stage and, behind it, four floors of backstage area and dressing rooms.

Makarova was rehearsing when Mikhail appeared from backstage to watch her. Note that despite the heat, which was overpowering that day, Mikhail was wearing his rubber suit.

Cynthia Harvey and Elizabeth Ashton, of the American Ballet Theatre, after a rehearsal at the Louvre. Lines and shadows intermingle. Cynthia Harvey is not exercising, but simply resting her leg. Dancers think nothing of resting their legs in such positions, as a way of relaxing. Try doing it sometime on your dining-room table while you chat with a friend. You'll see it's not as easy as it looks. . . . Summer 1977.

One evening, about two hours before a scheduled performance, I decided to go to the amphitheater in the Louvre to rest. When I arrived I heard some lovely music coming from the loudspeaker—Russian folkloric music. Intrigued, I moved closer and saw that it was Mikhail Baryshnikov playing the piano. I took out my camera and began to take pictures, moving in slightly with each successive shot. There was a pretty young lady standing next to him when I began, but when she saw me she discreetly vanished. I kept on taking pictures until I was onstage a few feet from him, and he kept on playing, seemingly oblivious of my presence. For the last pictures I took I actually climbed onto the piano. When I had taken my seventieth photo he rose, smiled, and asked me to stop.

The picture you see here shows Baryshnikov's reflection in the lid of the piano. Summer 1977.

Charles Ward, a principal dancer of the American Ballet Theatre, during a rehearsal at the Louvre. After this tour, Ward took a leave of absence from the company to star in Bob Fosse's Broadway musical *Dancin'*. Summer 1977.

The wings of the Louvre amphitheater, about half an hour before a performance was to begin during the American Ballet Theatre's 1977 tour. I was struck by the prisonlike bleakness of this backstage view, and by the obvious symbolism: dance too is a prison.

Jean-Pierre Bonnefous during a makeup session in his dressing room. New York, 1976.

Close-up of Jean-Pierre Bonnefous.

Patricia McBride before a performance of George Balanchine's *Jewels* at the New York State Theater. Same new shoes in the background. For Patricia, as for many female dancers, the makeup session is a real ceremony. They sometimes arrive as much as an hour and a half before the ballet begins, and labor over their makeup, especially their eyes, which are all-important. Ballerinas, by the way, all wear false eyelashes onstage, which gives them that doelike look. May 1976.

Close-up of Patricia McBride, a few minutes
before a performance.

Patricia McBride. Third stage of the makeup session prior to the May 1976 performance of *Jewels*, in which Patricia danced "rubies."

Peter Martins, a principal dancer of the New York City Ballet, before a performance of Balanchine's *Agon*. He allowed me to photograph him one day while he was finishing getting dressed. Peter's head, at this angle and in this light, struck me as that of a Greek sculpture. Paris, 1978.

Fernando Bujones, a principal dancer of the
American Ballet Theatre. Taken at City
Center. New York, January 1977.

Fanchon Cordell, of the American Ballet
Theatre, a few minutes before going onstage
in *La Bayadère*. Paris, 1976.

Close-up of Fanchon Cordell as she prepares to go onstage, in Paris, for a performance of *La Bayadère*. She had completed her warm-ups, was completely made up, and ready to go on, when I caught her in this lovely light.

Linda Homek, of the New York City Ballet, backstage at the Théâtre des Champs-Élysées. This too was taken minutes before a performance. Here she is running through the steps "piqué-jeté-fini-arabesque" that she will be repeating moments later onstage. Paris, November 1976.

View of the backstage of the Théâtre des Champs-Élysées in Paris during a performance of a ballet by Paolo Bortoluzzi, the great Italian dancer. Those backstage were clearly mesmerized by the ballet's beauty, and everyone's attention was riveted on Bortoluzzi's performance.

The dancer in this picture is leaning on one of the loudspeakers backstage. For these performances, as for many, there is no live orchestra. The music was all prerecorded for the ballet company's European tour. Especially when traveling, it is far easier for a company to carry several tapes than to transport a full orchestra, especially when contemporary music is involved.

Peter Martins, in the wings of the Monte Carlo Theater, winter 1978, during a performance of *Agon*. Peter and Suzanne Farrell were invited by the Ballet du Grand Théâtre de Genève—as guest stars with the company for certain specific roles. Here, Peter is watching two stars of the Geneva company perform the pas de deux that he usually performs with Suzanne in New York.

The Ballet du Grand Théâtre de Genève is, by the way, a European branch of the New York City Ballet. It was formed by Balanchine, and as with its New York counterpart is choreographed mainly by him. Therefore, when New York City Ballet stars are invited as guests to perform with the Geneva company, they need very little rehearsal, since the steps of the ballet are identical.

Note here that Peter Martins is wearing a boxer's robe, and like a boxer he has his name emblazoned in bold letters on the back.

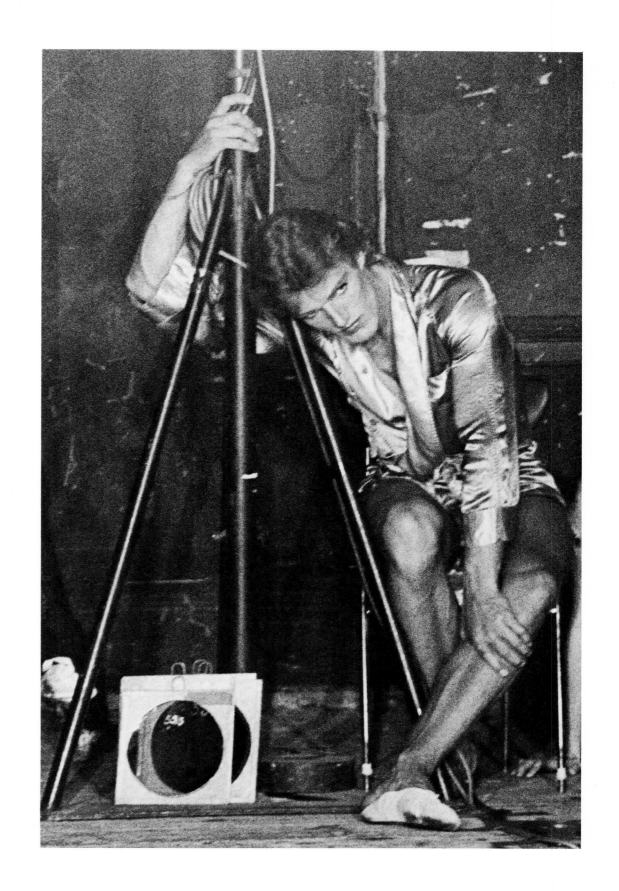

Violette Verdy, during a Paris tour by the New York City Ballet, at the Théâtre des Champs-Élysées in November 1976. Violette had just finished her solo in Jerome Robbins' *Dances at a Gathering*, and now, having donned her dressing gown, is watching the other dancers.

This was Violette's last performance as a dancer. Shortly after this tour she was named head of the Paris Opéra.

Among all of Nature's artisans, the beaver, bee, and spider invariably display the qualities of courage and patience.

Mythology and history provide us with examples of animals real and imaginary. In a world situated somewhere between Mythology and Nature, the unicorn and centaur were born. And the dancer.

His birth: artificial.

His actions: conscious, re-created, reconsidered.

His freedom: carefully acquired, calculated, chosen.

His habitat: backstage, halfway between the jungle and the zoo.

In the jungle, we are fascinated by the freedom and beauty of wild animals in their natural surroundings. In the zoo, we admire them but we also feel sorry for them. The Dance of Life is Freedom.

Penelope devoted herself to repeating the same act each day, over and over again; speeded up, the intensity of that act explodes into Dance.

The extraordinary demands of practice and preparation last a dancer his or her entire life.

The quintessential moment—a distillation of all the others, so short, once again become as natural as the immemorial "pasts" of free animals—is the Stage.

And Dance—whether onstage or backstage—is intensity wrought from within. And what greater gift can one offer, at once completely public yet also completely private.

—Violette Verdy

Suzanne Farrell backstage at the Théâtre de Monte Carlo. Suzanne is made up and ready to go onstage; here she is doing final warm-ups before dancing in *Chaconne*.

This theater, by the way, is an extraordinary one, designed by the same architect who designed the Paris Opéra. All the older European theaters have a gentle aura about them; even backstage, there is none of the bleakness that one so often finds in the wings and corridors of the newer, American theaters. Easter 1978.

Three members of the Geneva Ballet watching with awe as their two American guest stars, Suzanne Farrell and Peter Martins, dance *Chaconne*.

The girls, who have just finished dancing *Agon*, are: Stephanie Herman (partly hidden by the pole), a principal dancer; Anne Brossier, sitting on the piano; and Mandy Bennett. Monte Carlo, April 1978.

The dressing room of the Théâtre de Monte Carlo. The dancers have just finished the ballet *Serenade*, and are getting ready for *Western Symphony*. Spring 1978.

Tutu and tunic. Taken at the Théâtre de Monte Carlo during a performance. The tutu is a costume for the ballet *Western Symphony*, and the tunic for *Agon*, both choreographed by Balanchine. Spring 1978.

"Ladies and Gentlemen, onstage, please. Three minutes." This picture, taken in the corridors of the Théâtre de Monte Carlo just before a performance, shows the wardrobe mistress taking a stitch in a dancer's costume. Tradition calls for the stitches to be taken on the costume after the dancer has donned it, for it gives the dancer a feeling that the costume and she are one. It is also customary for her to tear or cut the stitch after the performance. 1978.

Tutus, Paris. Small talk just before a performance.

Suzanne Farrell's extraordinary look. In this 1978 picture, taken at the Théâtre de Monte Carlo, she is wearing her *Symphony in C* costume.

George Balanchine has often compared Suzanne's beauty to that of a cheetah, for like that creature she is very quick and strong, and also to that of a fish: like a fish, he says, she can swim—that is, dance—forever.

Portrait of Suzanne Farrell watching the ballet in the wings of the Théâtre de Monte Carlo, just moments before she is to go onstage. Spring 1978.

Janie Hetland, of the Geneva Ballet, looking for all the world like an animated doll as she watches the company's performance of *Symphony in C*.

Admiring glances by two members of the Geneva Ballet, Elizabeth Carr and Lisa Corbet, as they watch Suzanne Farrell and Peter Martins do their variations in the second movement. They are dressed for their roles in *Symphony in C*, which followed next on the program.

Anne Brossier, of the Geneva company, being prepared by the wardrobe mistress, just before going onstage in *Serenade*.

Natalia Makarova, one of the great stars of contemporary ballet, at the Palais des Sports. She was dancing in *Les Sylphides* with Rudolf Nureyev for the first time in several years, and here, looking more like a little ballerina at her first ballet-school performance than like an international star, she watches a variation of the ballet, during a dress rehearsal. Paris, late January 1977.

Anne Brossier, of the Geneva Ballet, in the wings of the Théâtre de Monte Carlo watching a performance of *Serenade*. I was struck by the beauty of the ballerina, her position, and the ethereal quality about her as she watched. Spring 1978.

Tutus for *Serenade*.

Floris Alexander, a principal dancer of the Geneva company, catching his breath and drying himself off between two appearances in *Four Temperaments*. Monte Carlo, 1978.

Peter Martins and Suzanne Farrell take their bows after their performance. Brooklyn College, January 1977.